See and Draw

Faces

Copyright 2018 See and Draw

www.SeeAndDraw.com

To become a better artist or illustrator, it is recommended that you challenge yourself daily by attempting to draw a wide range of images of varying complexity.

Within this book, you will find XX pencil-drawn illustrations displayed on the left-hand pages and blank pages on the right-side to be used as a drawing surface.

This book makes a great gift for anyone who has shown an interest in learning to draw.

.

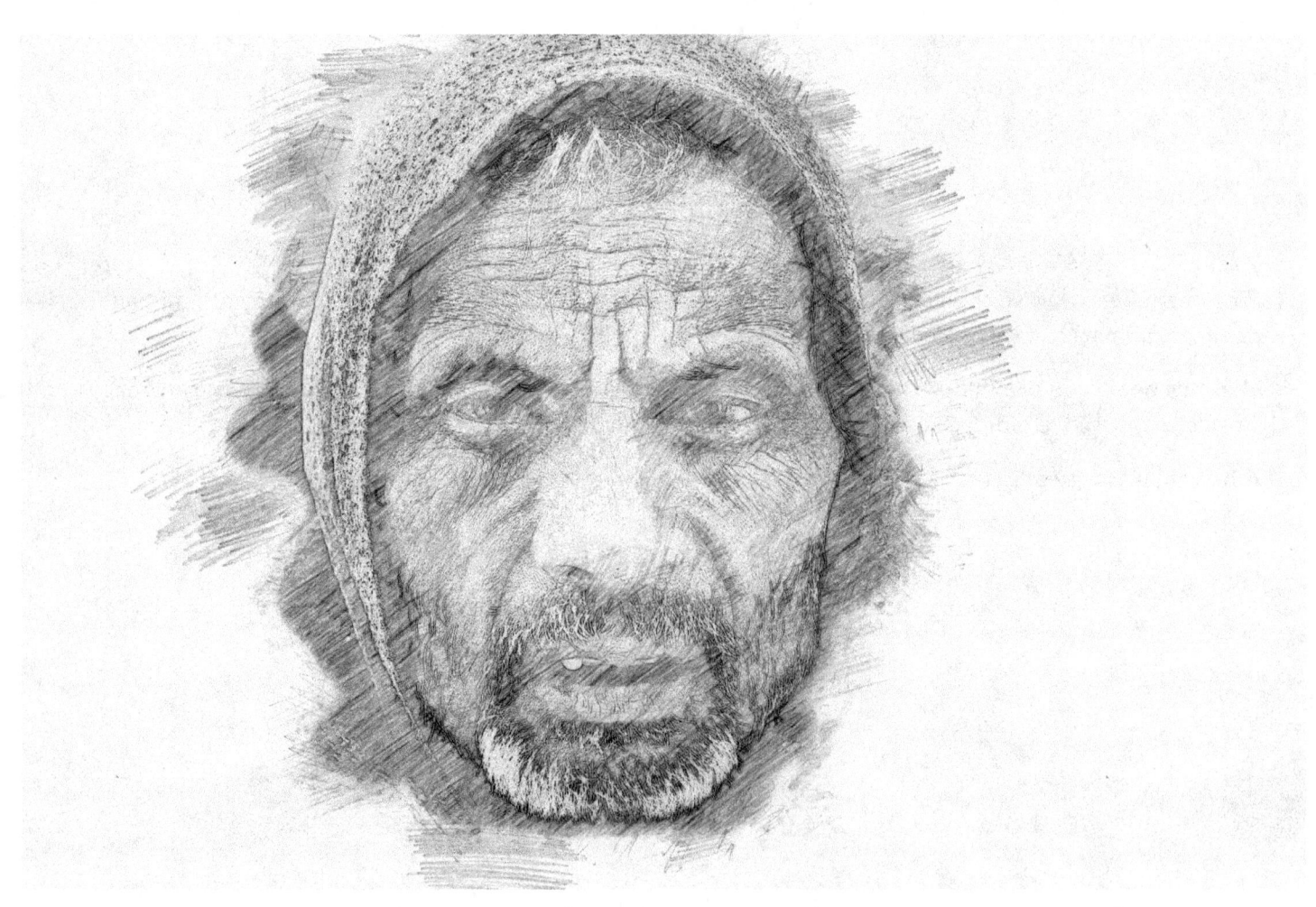

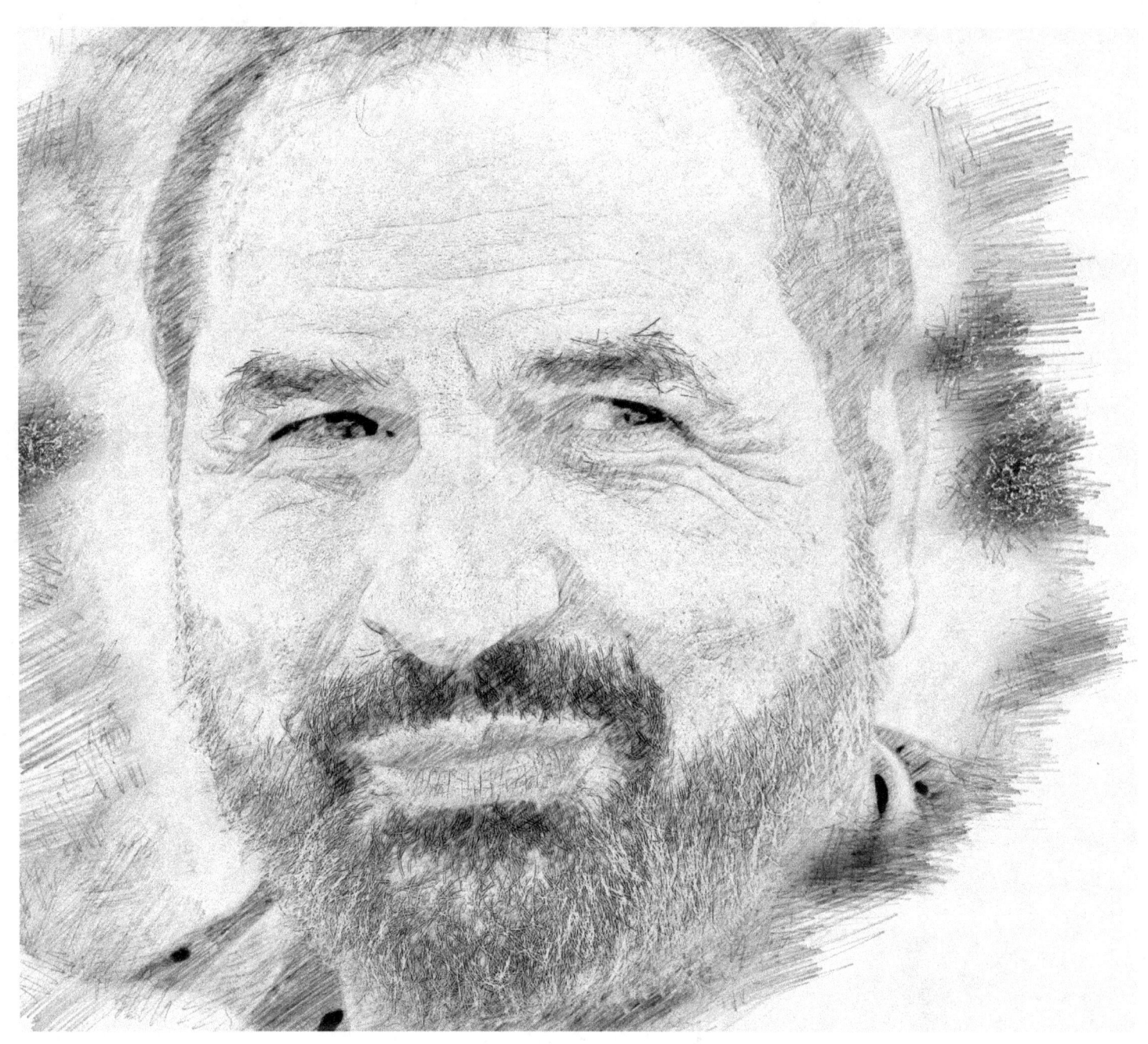

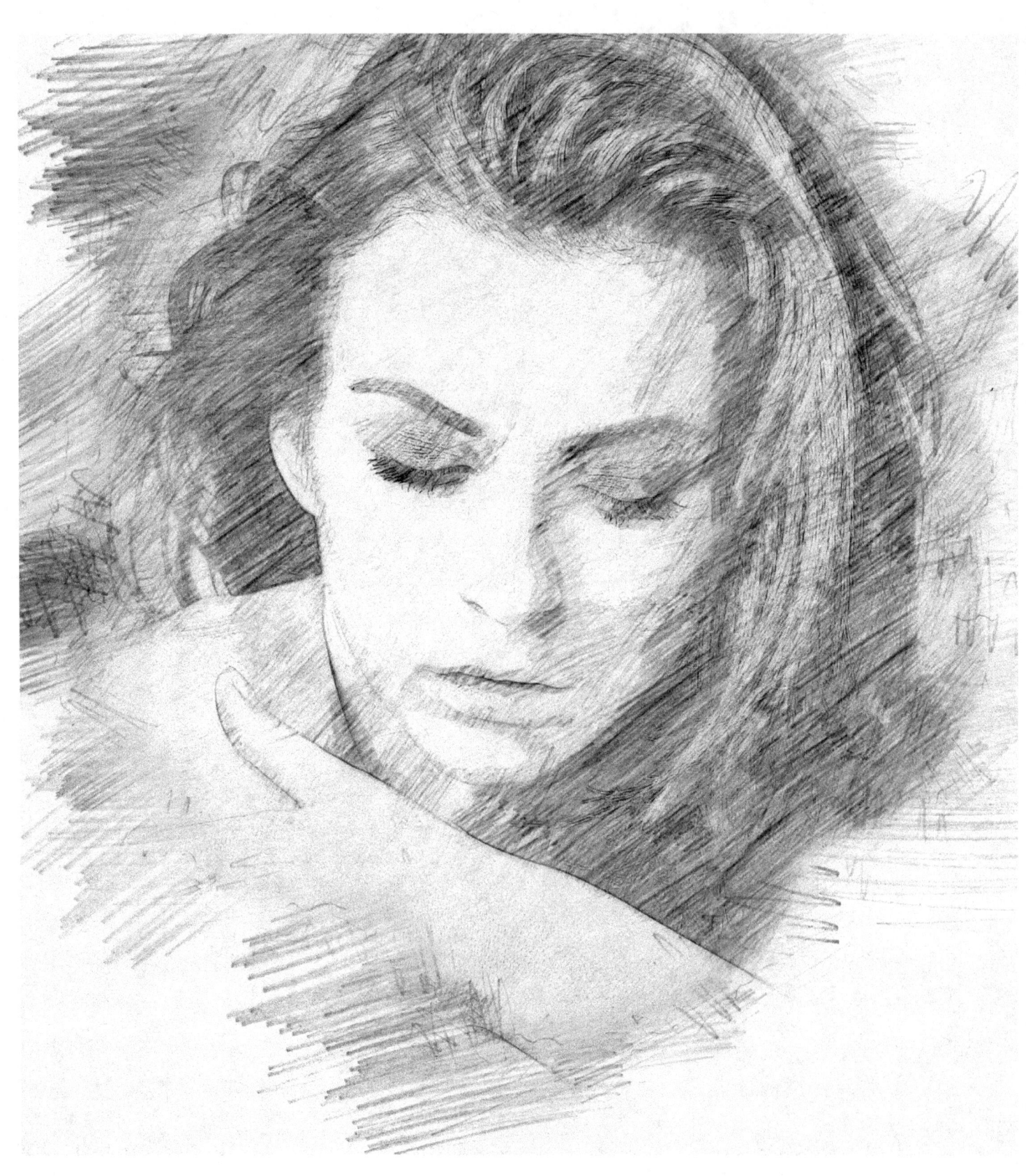

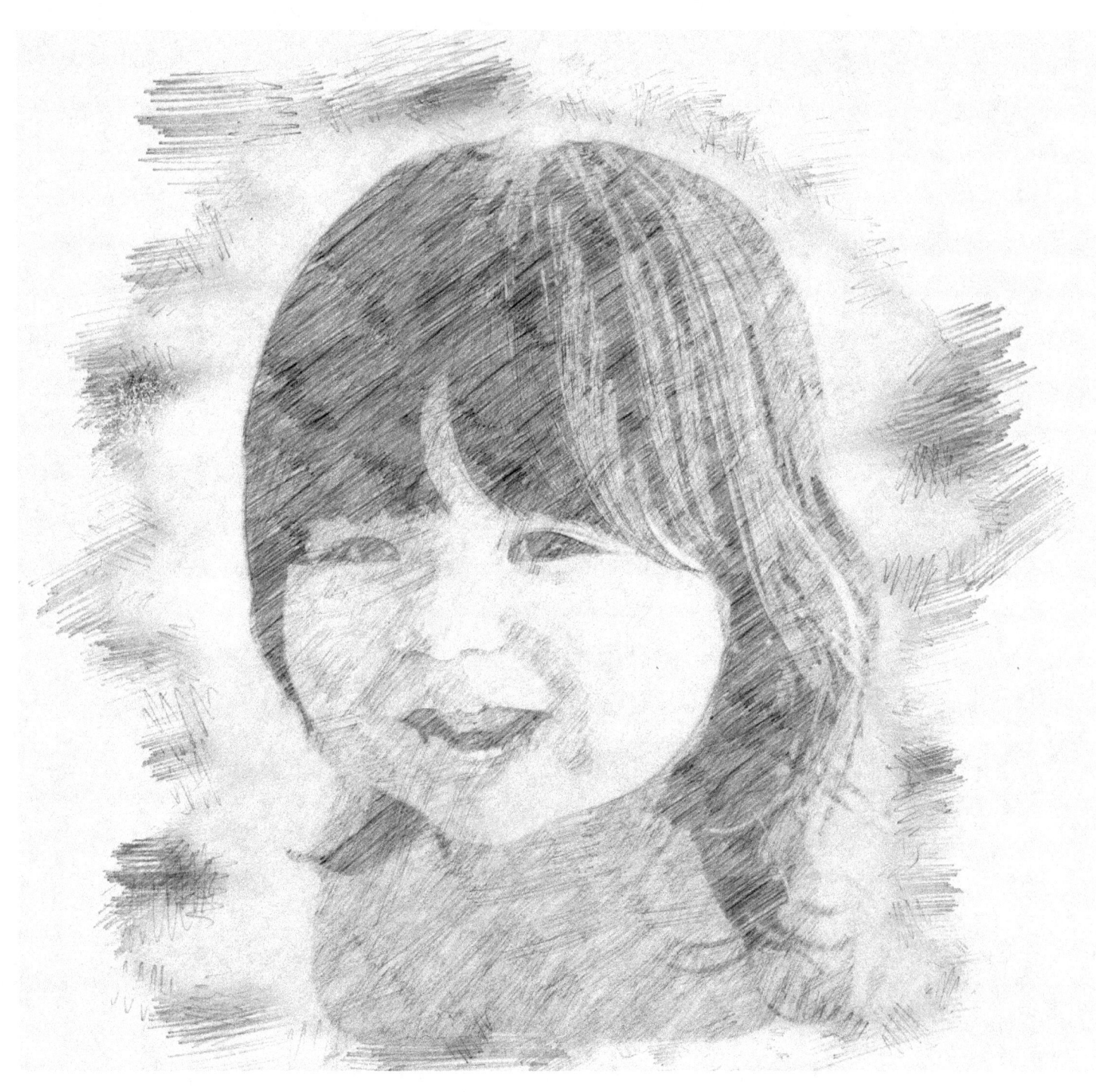

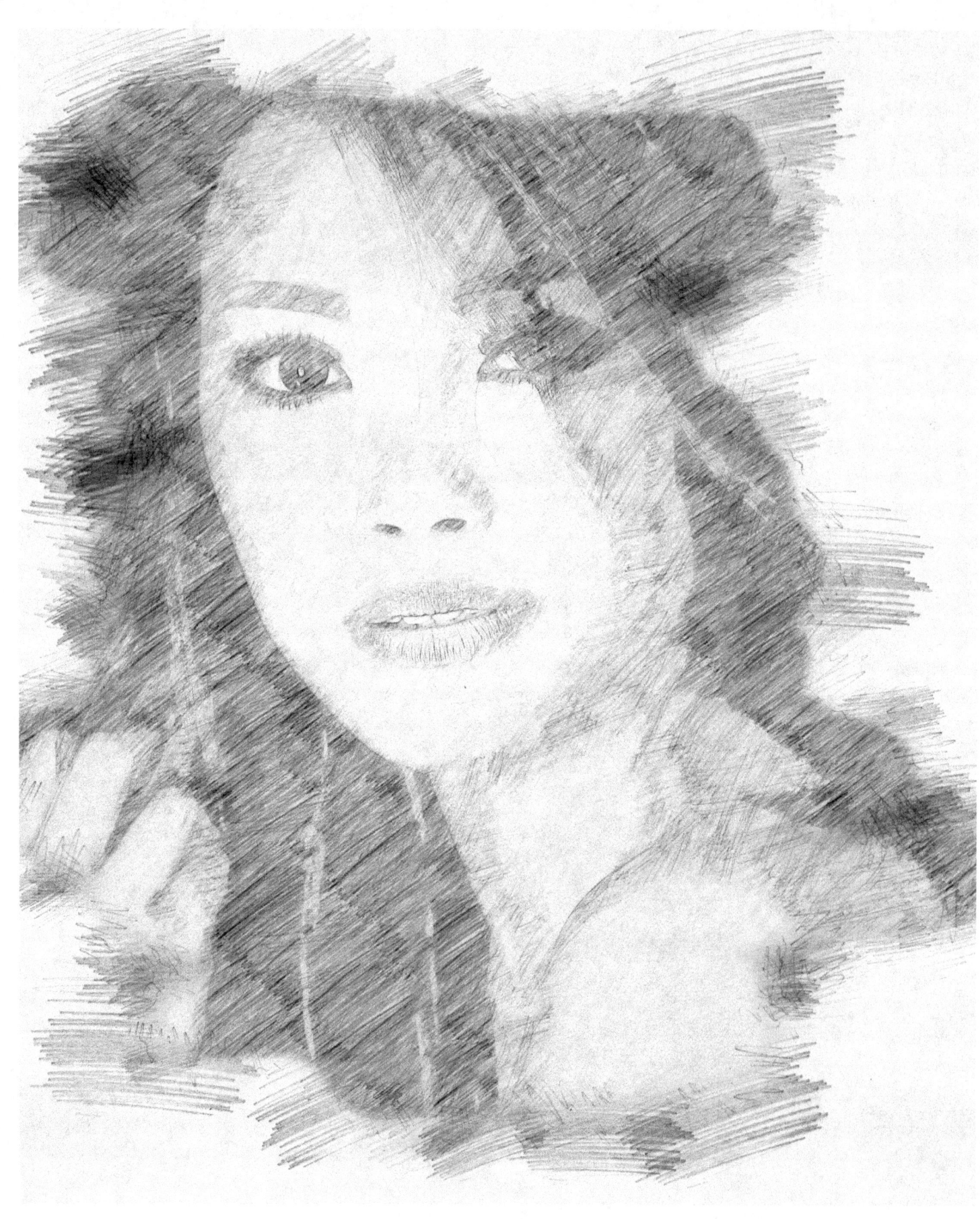

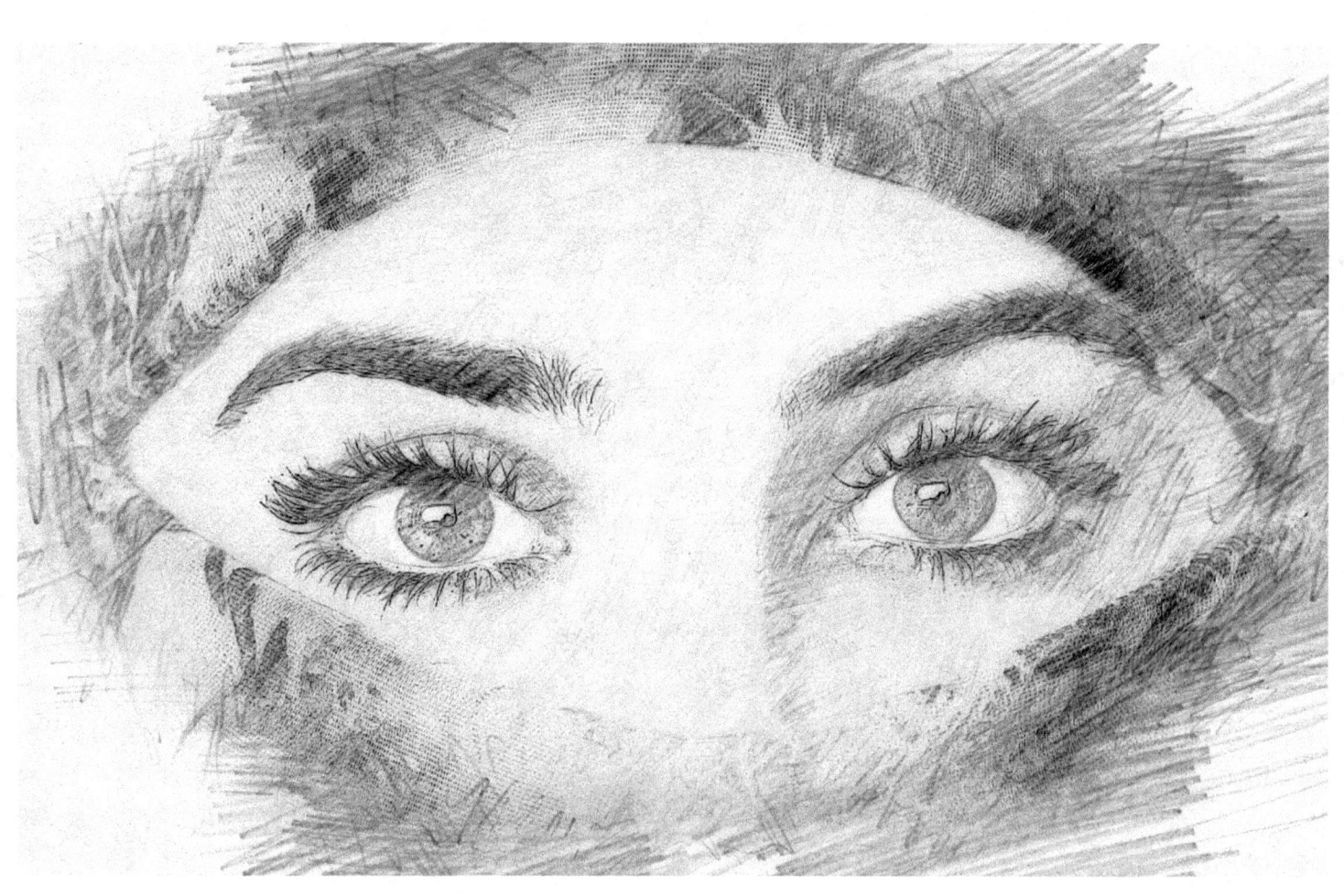

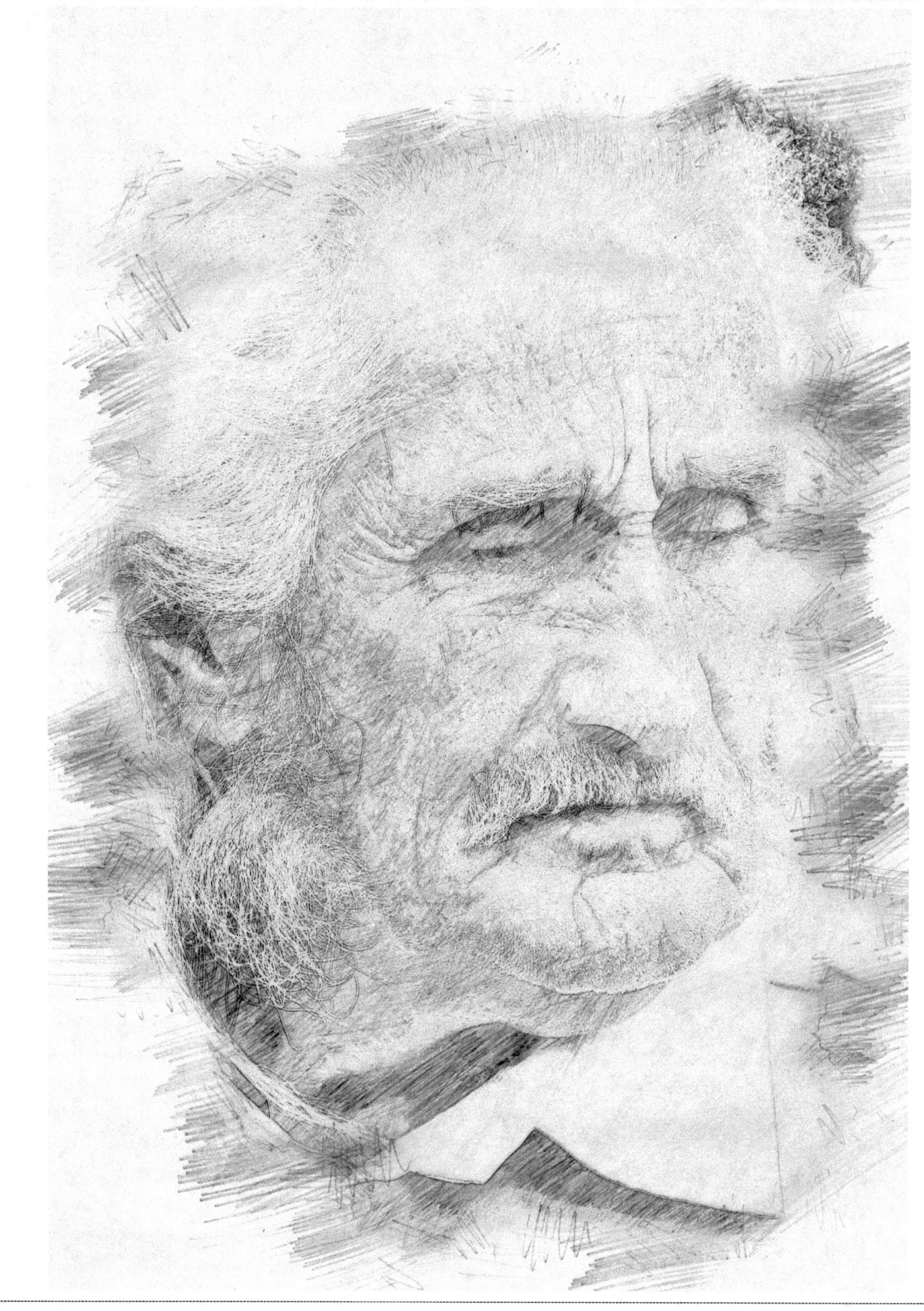

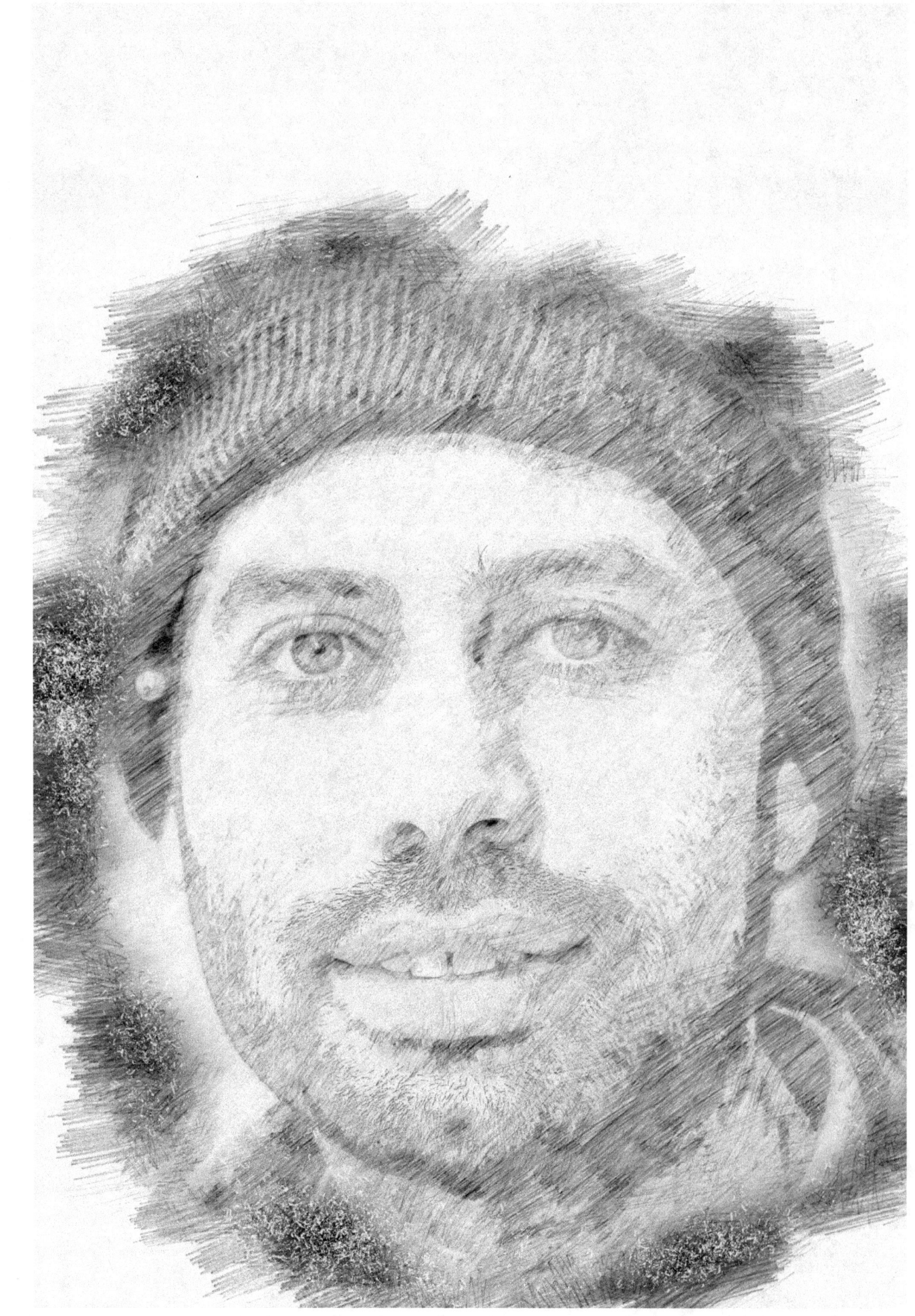

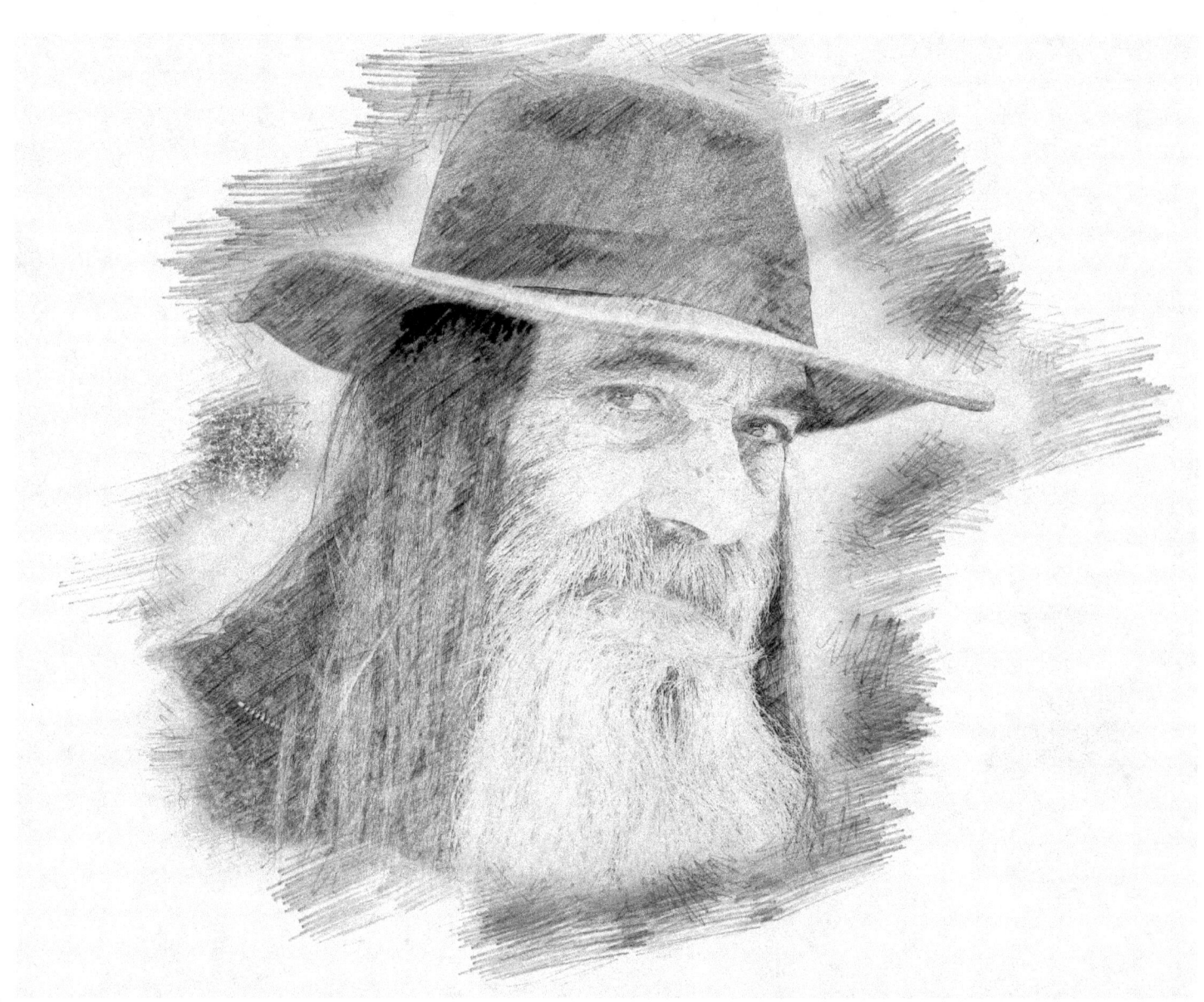

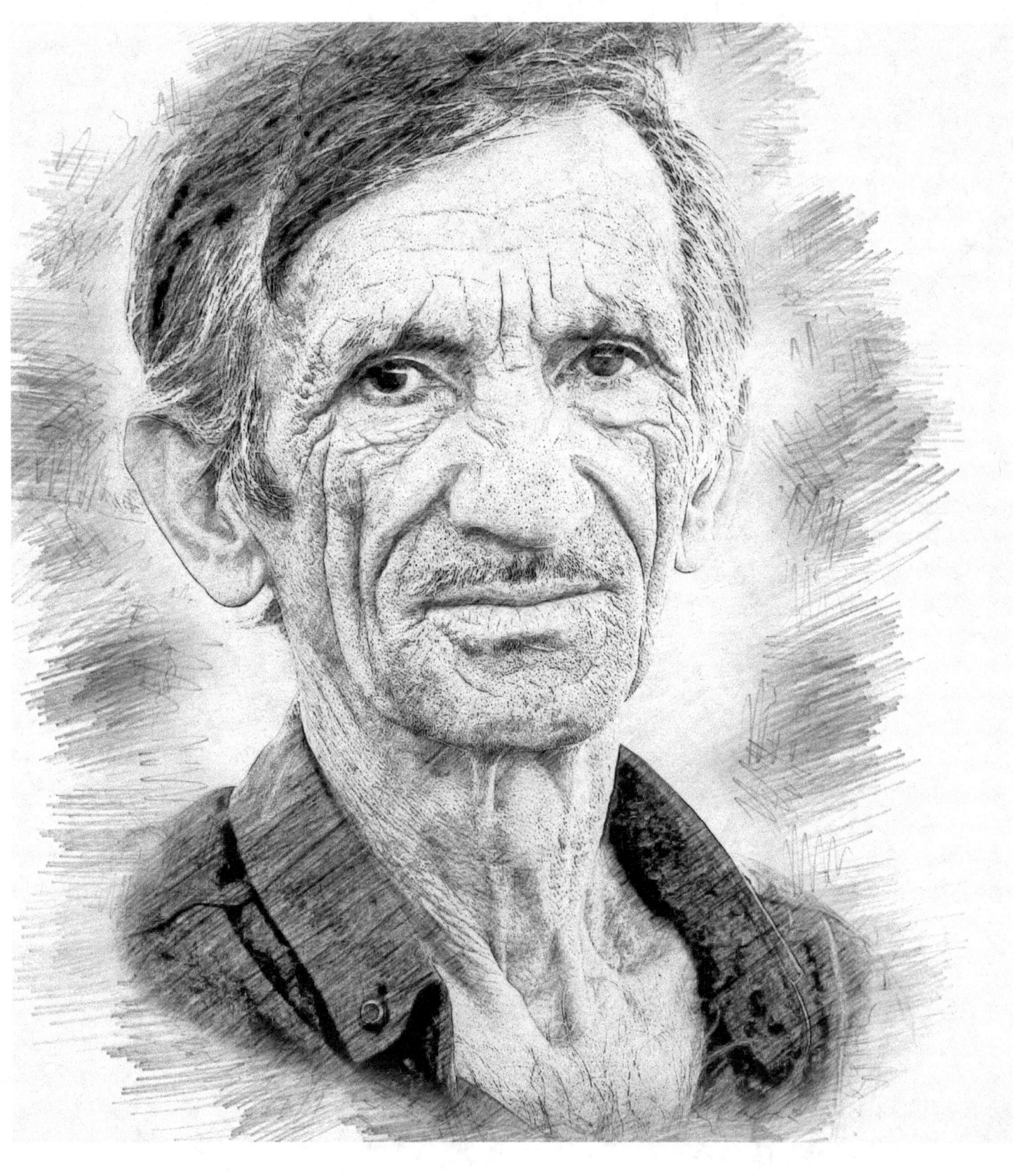

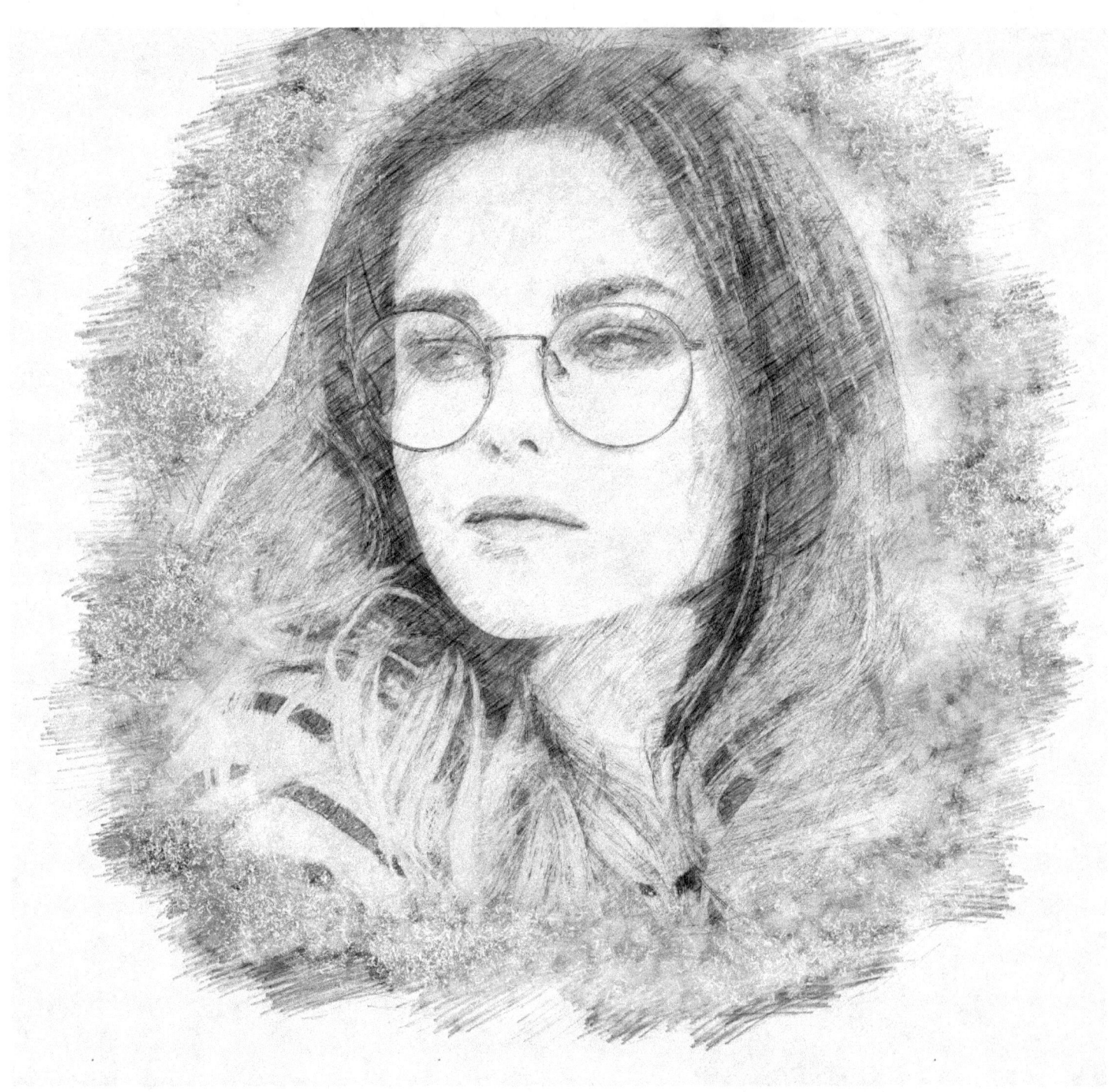

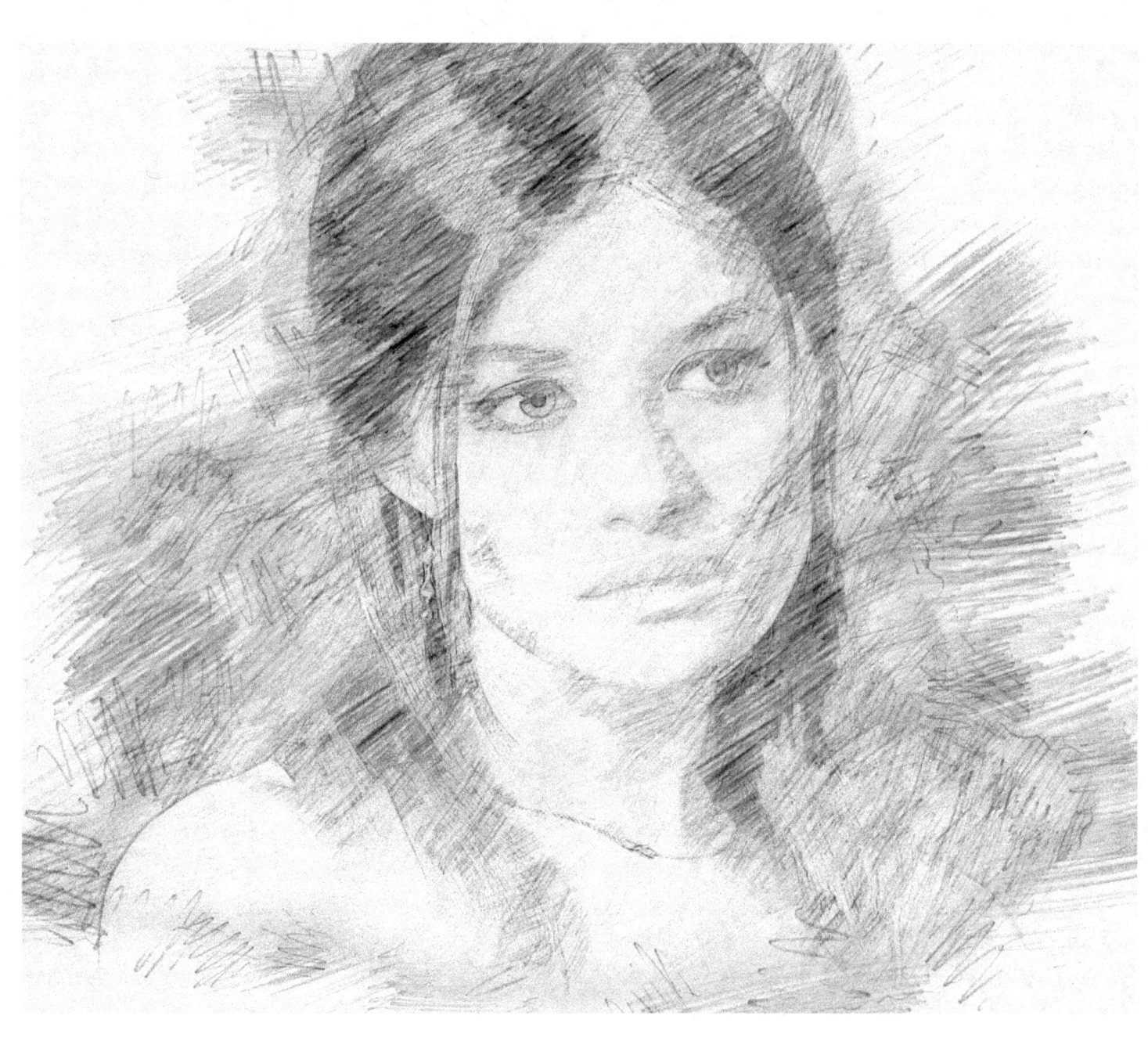

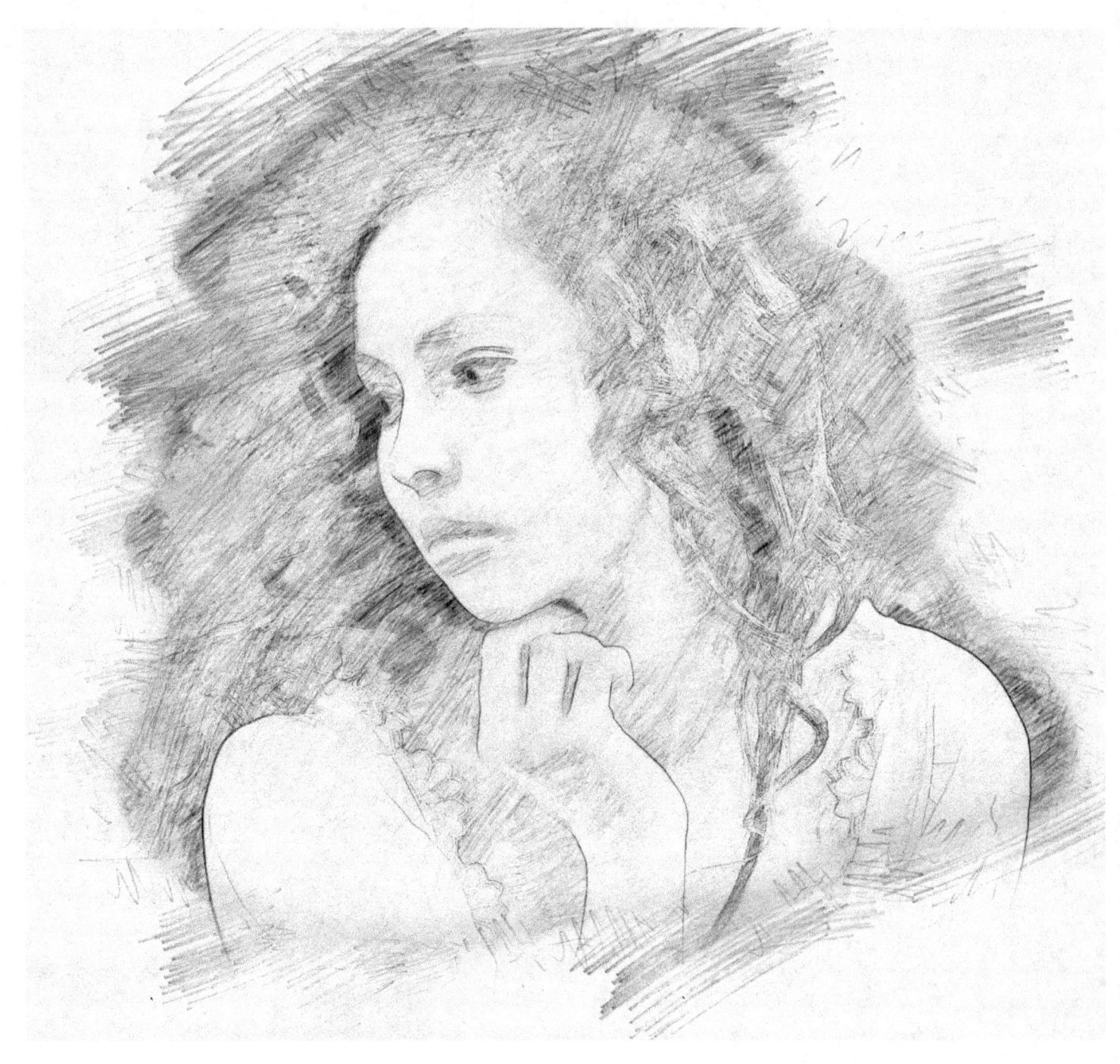

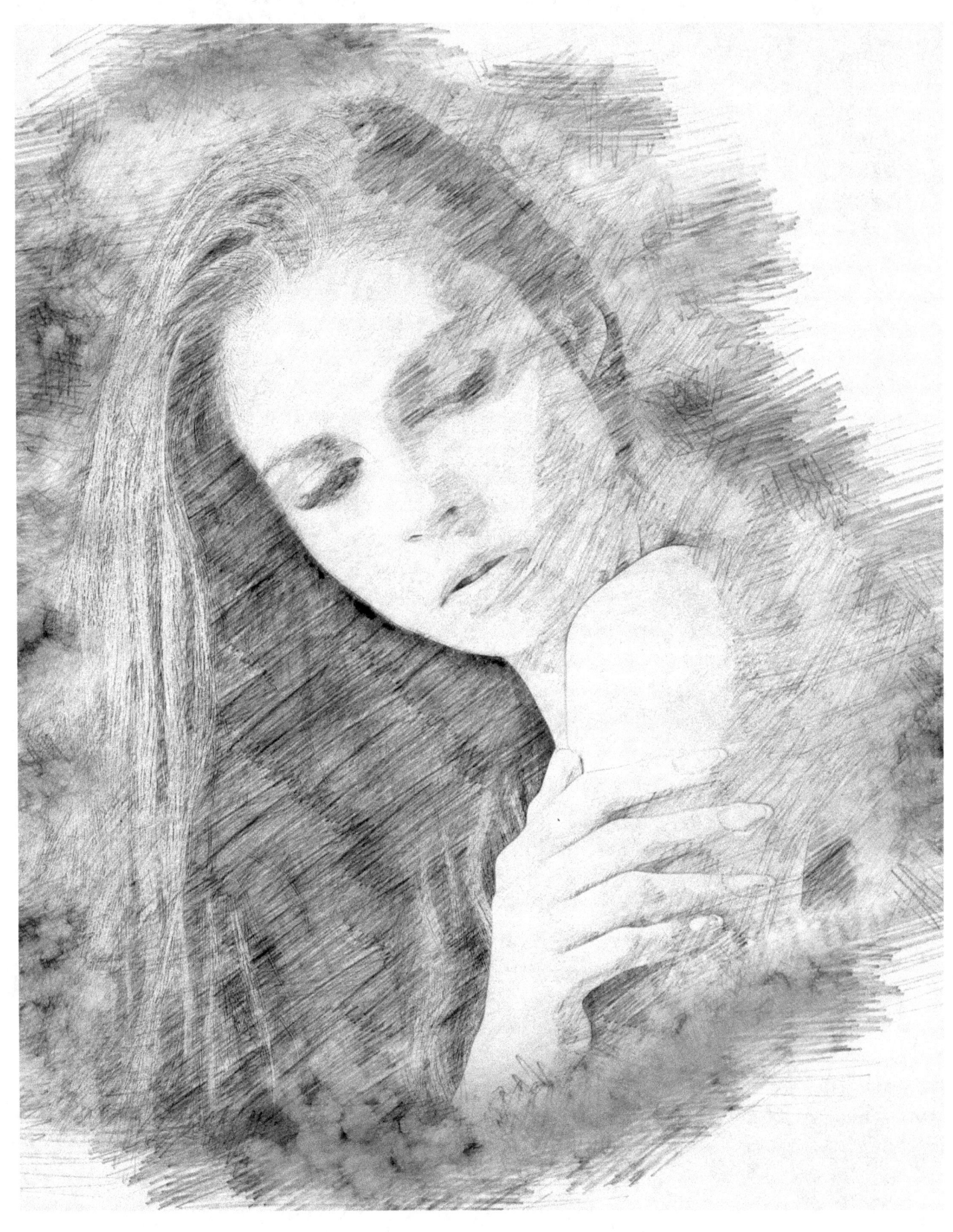

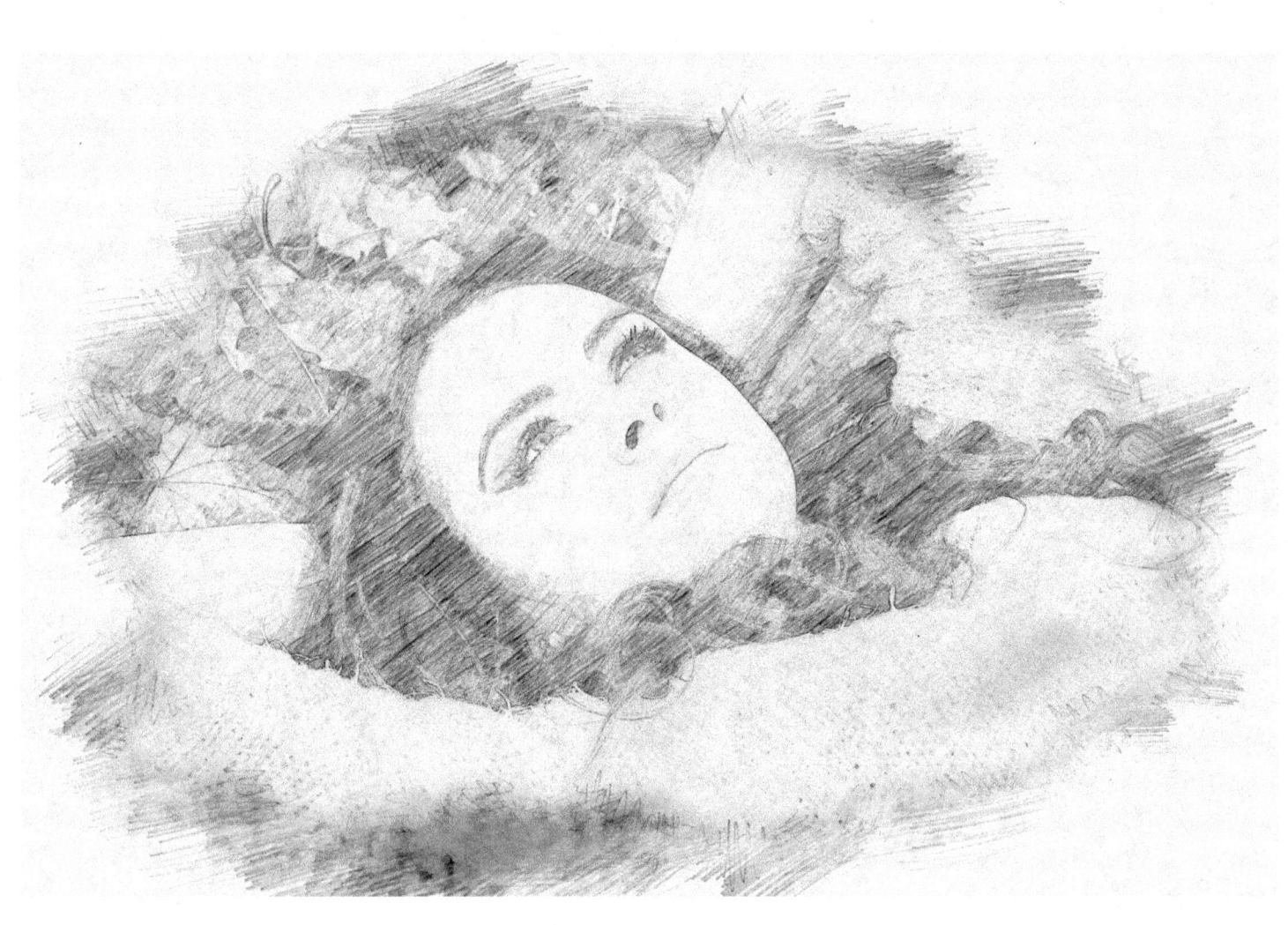

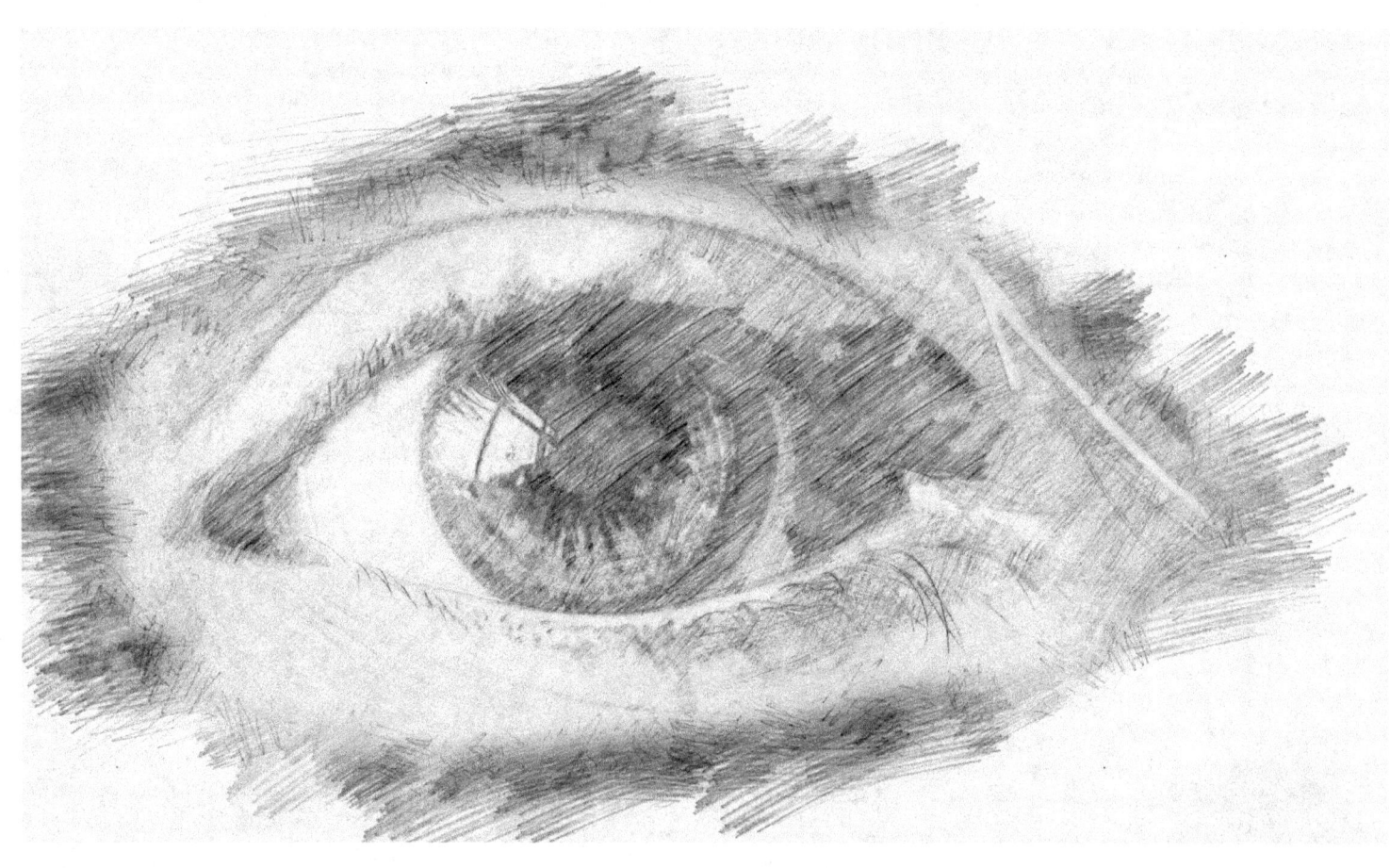

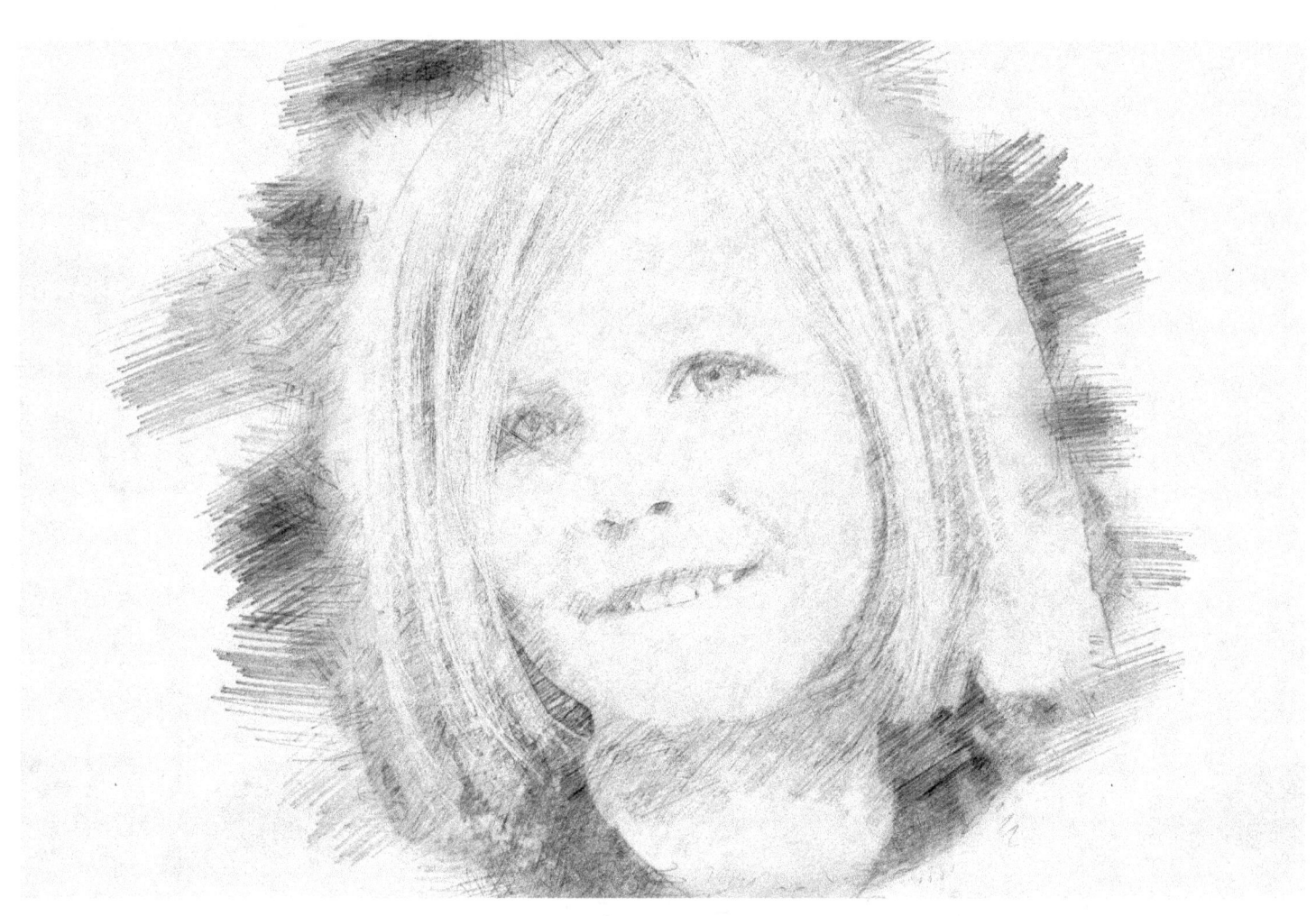

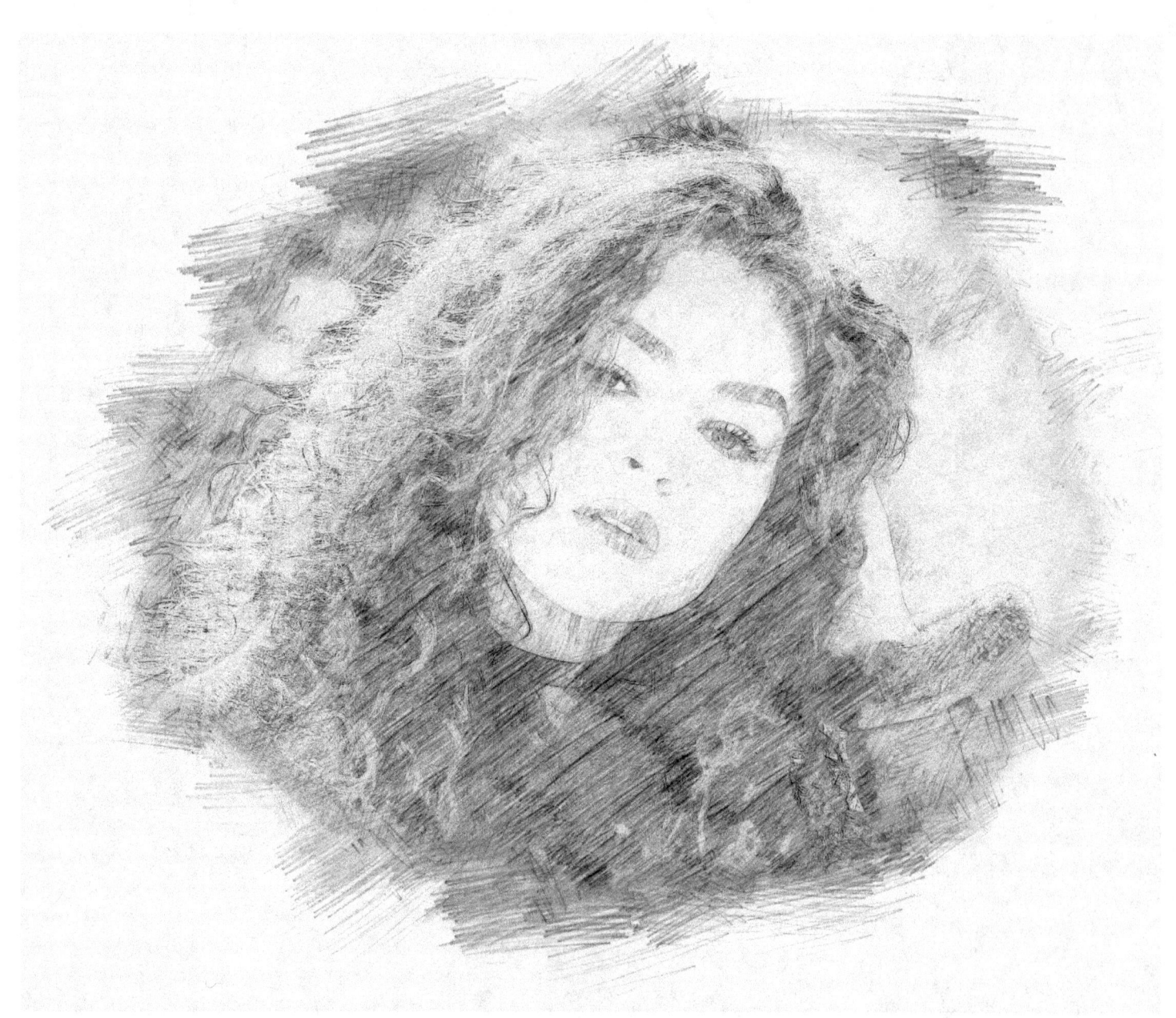

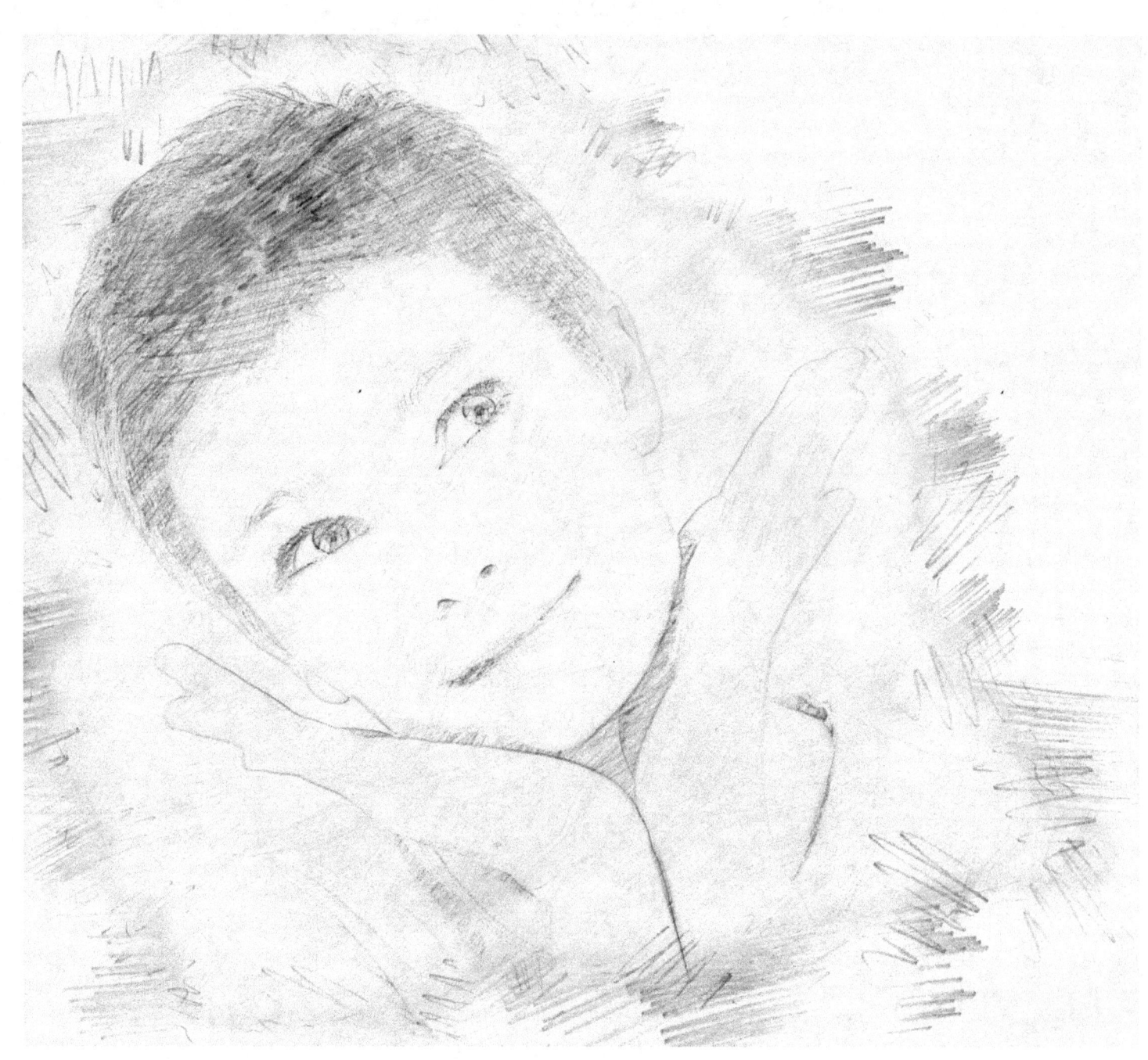

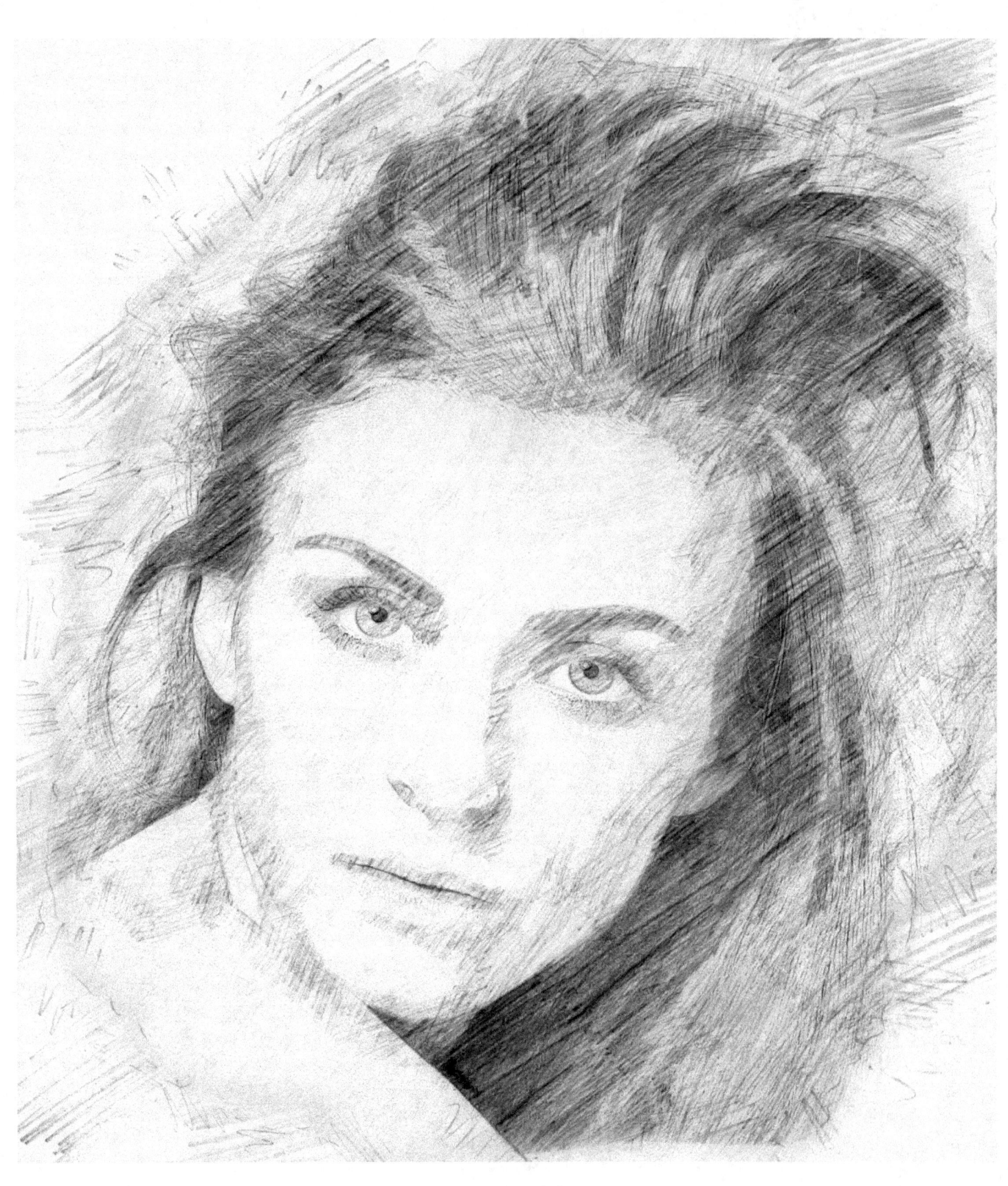

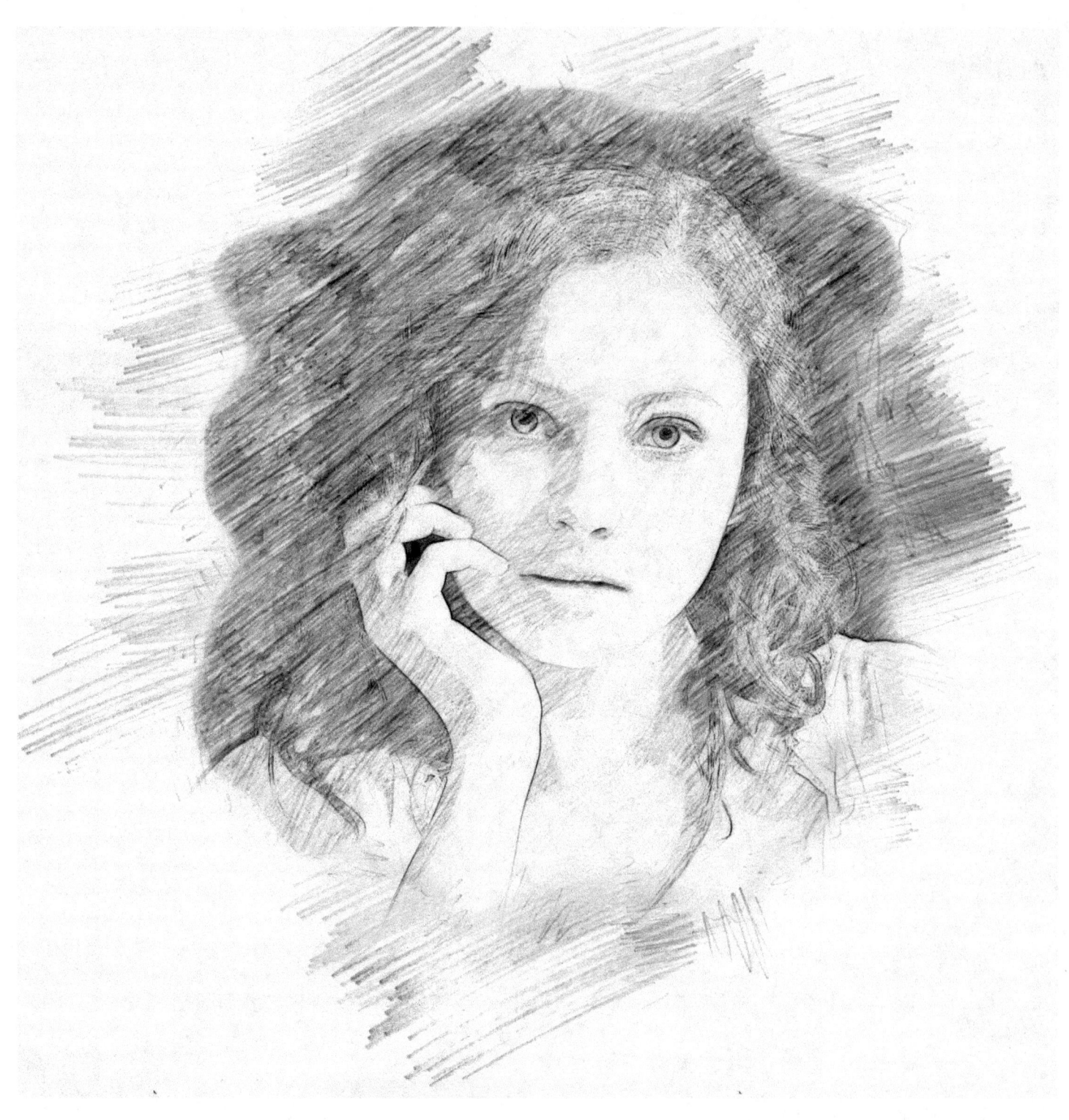

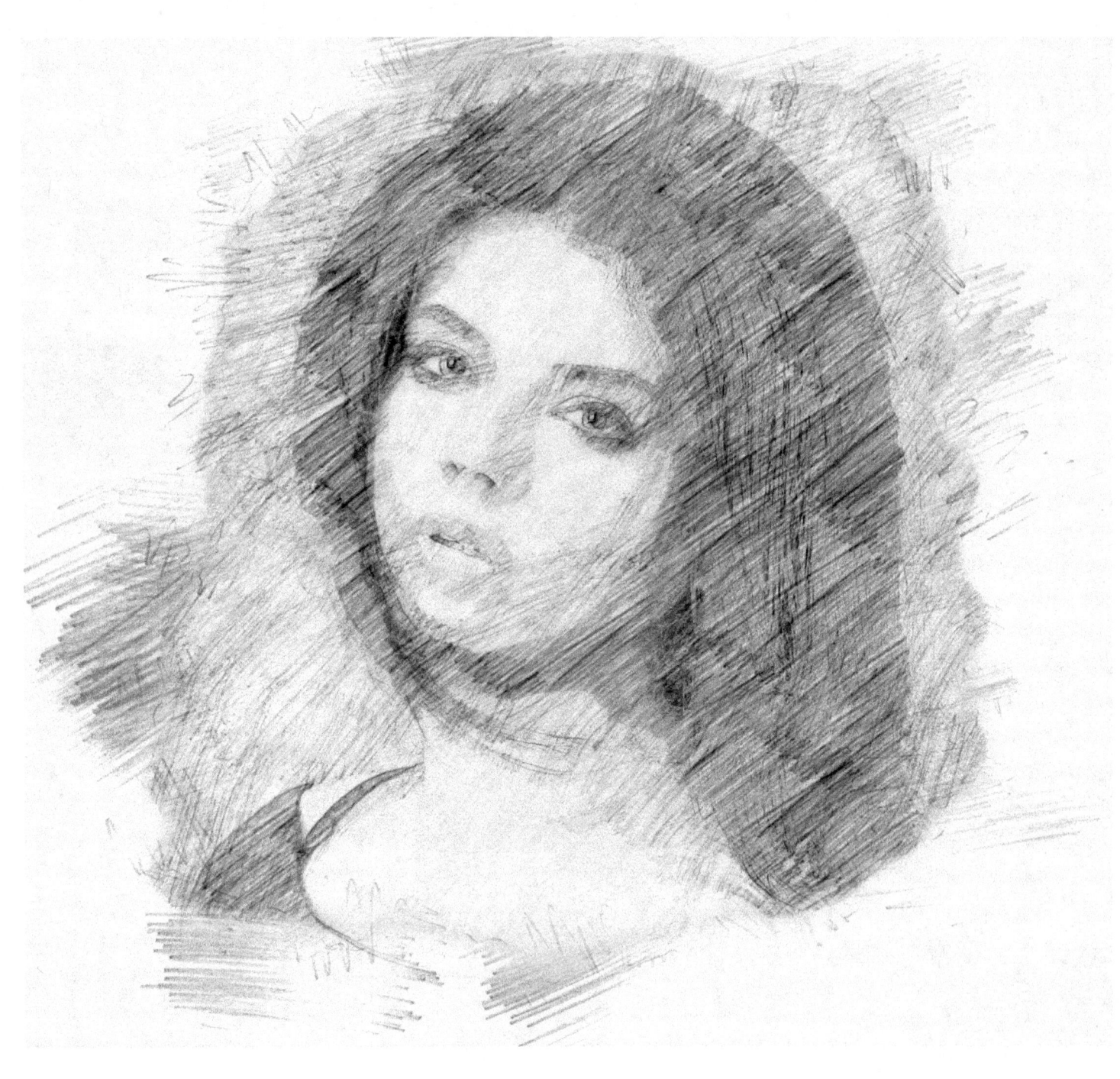

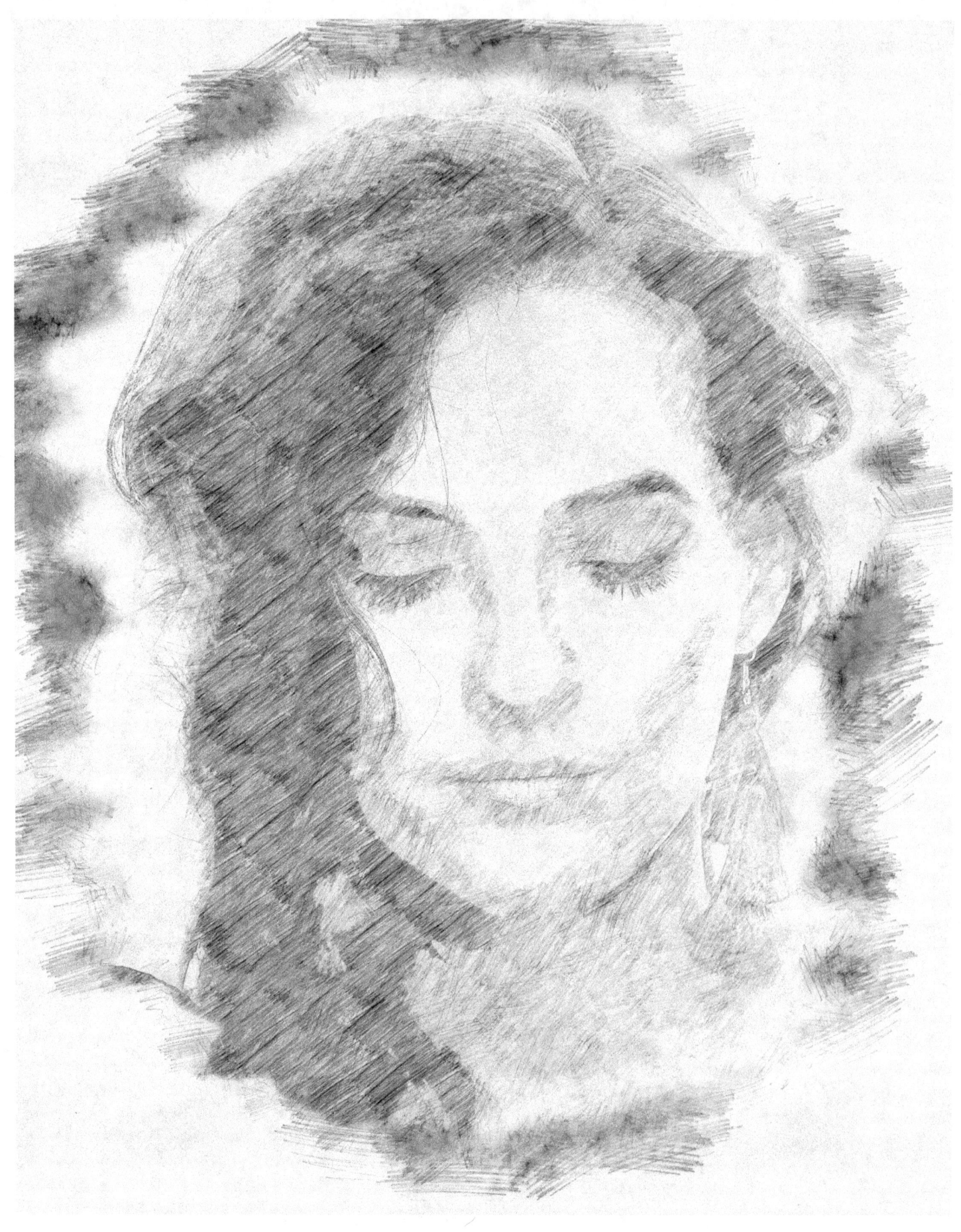

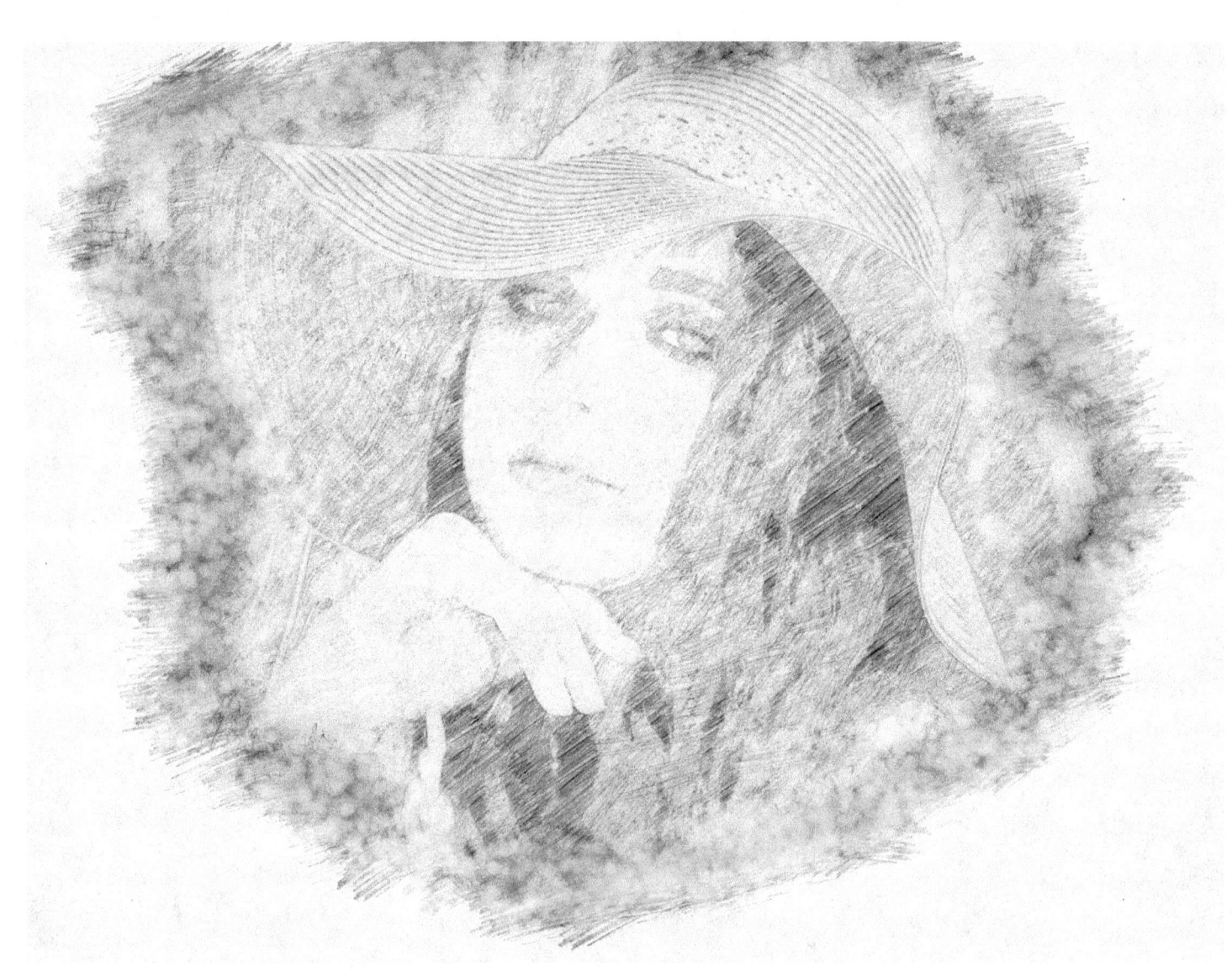

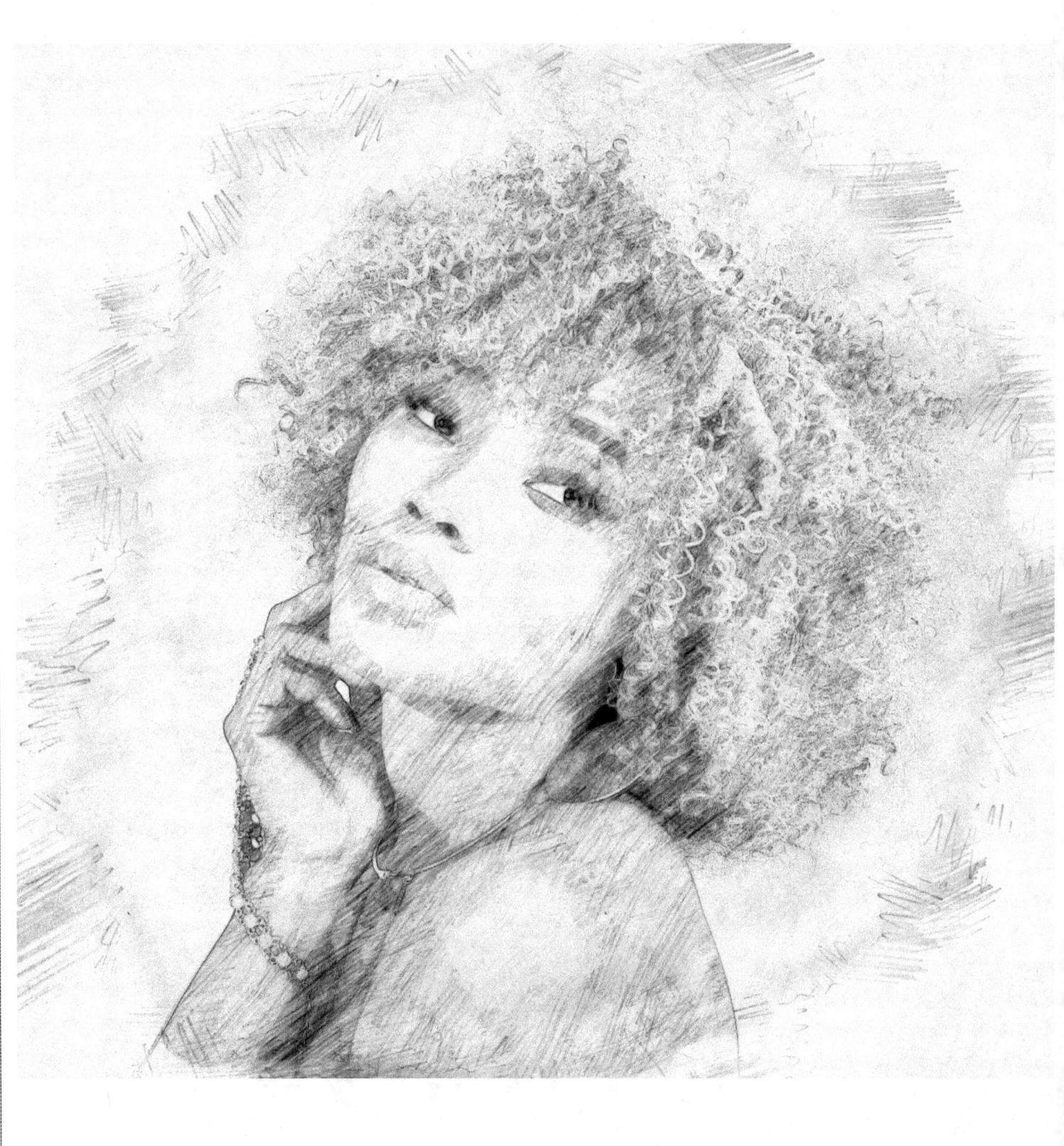

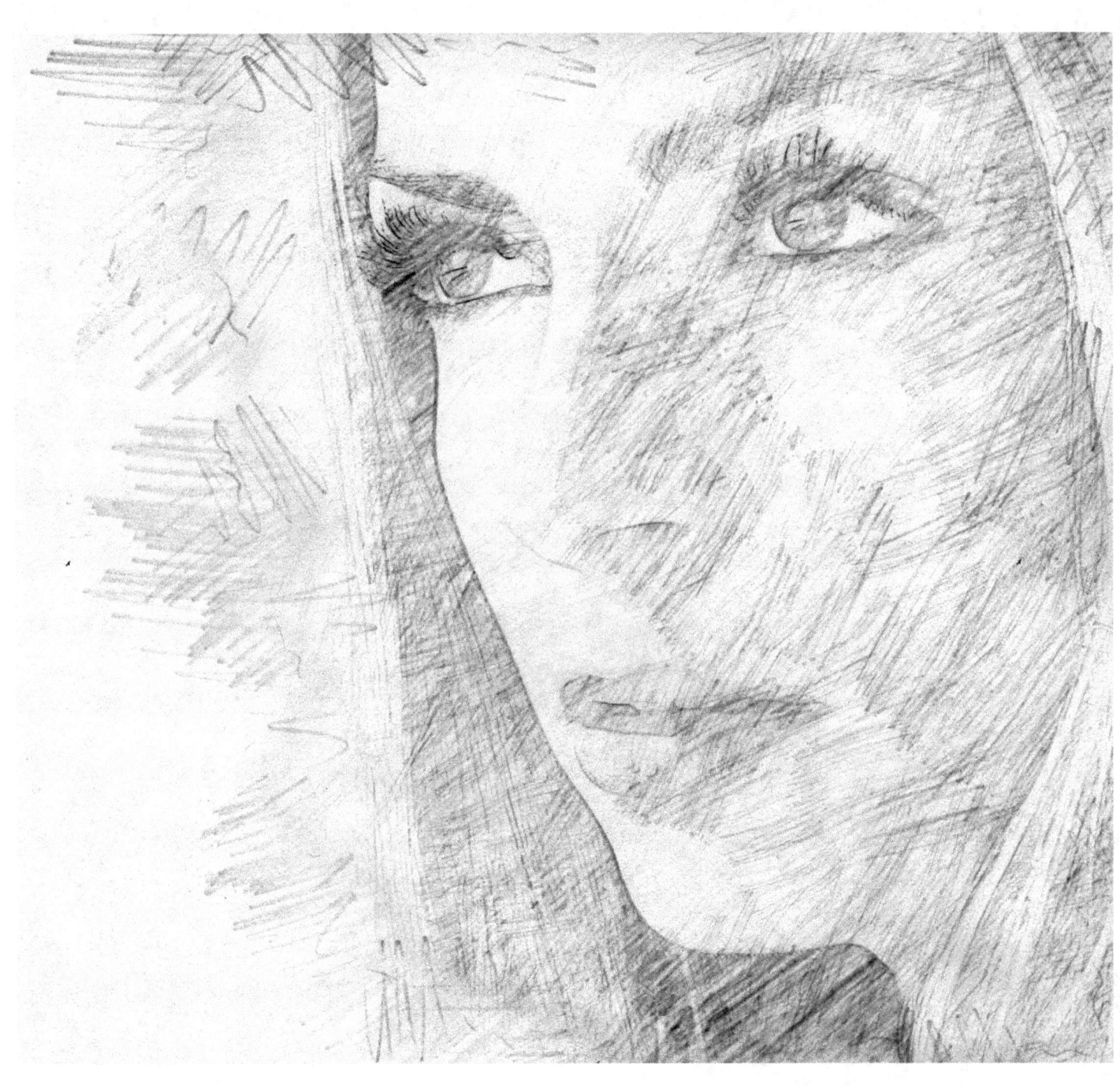

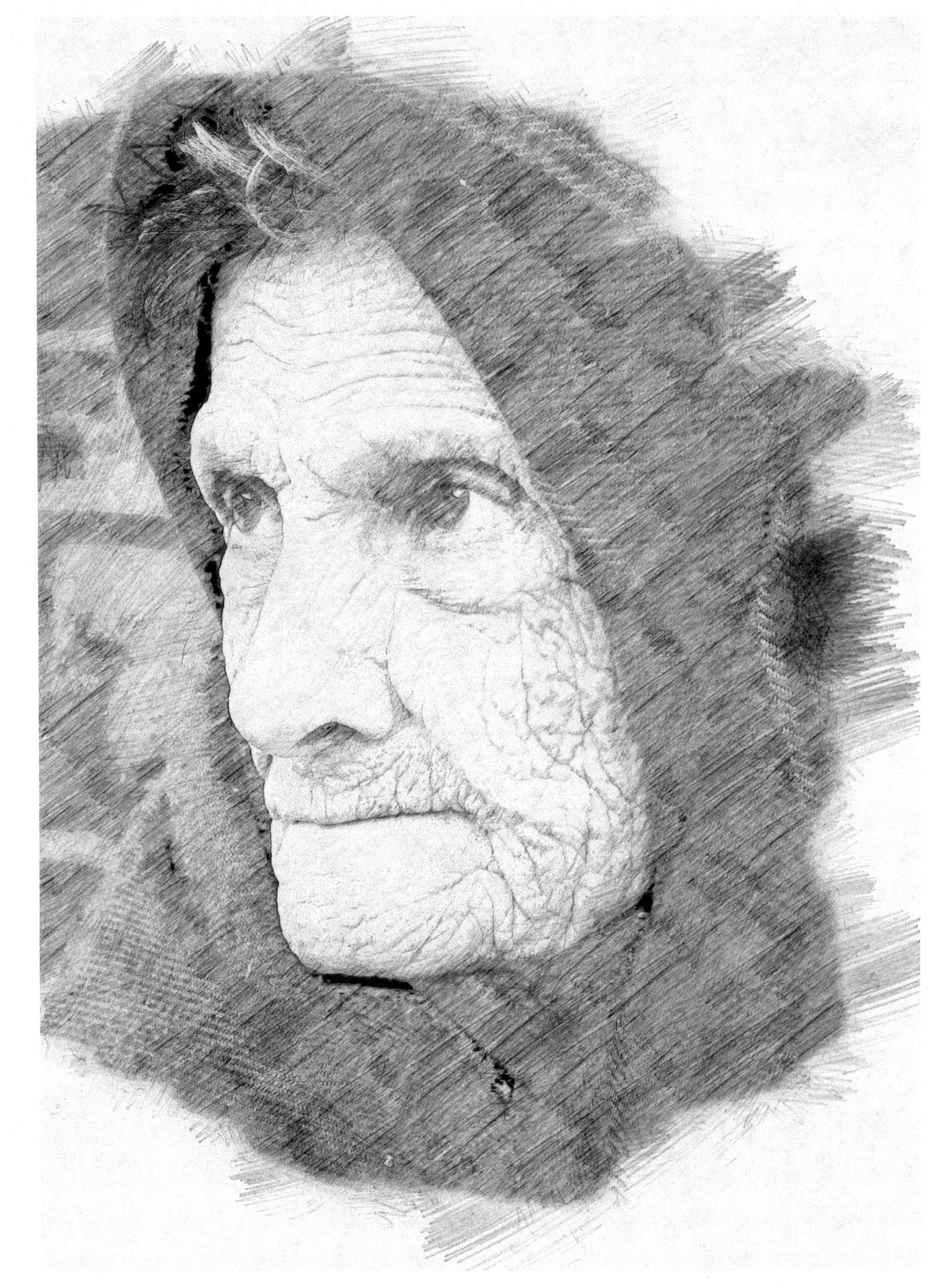

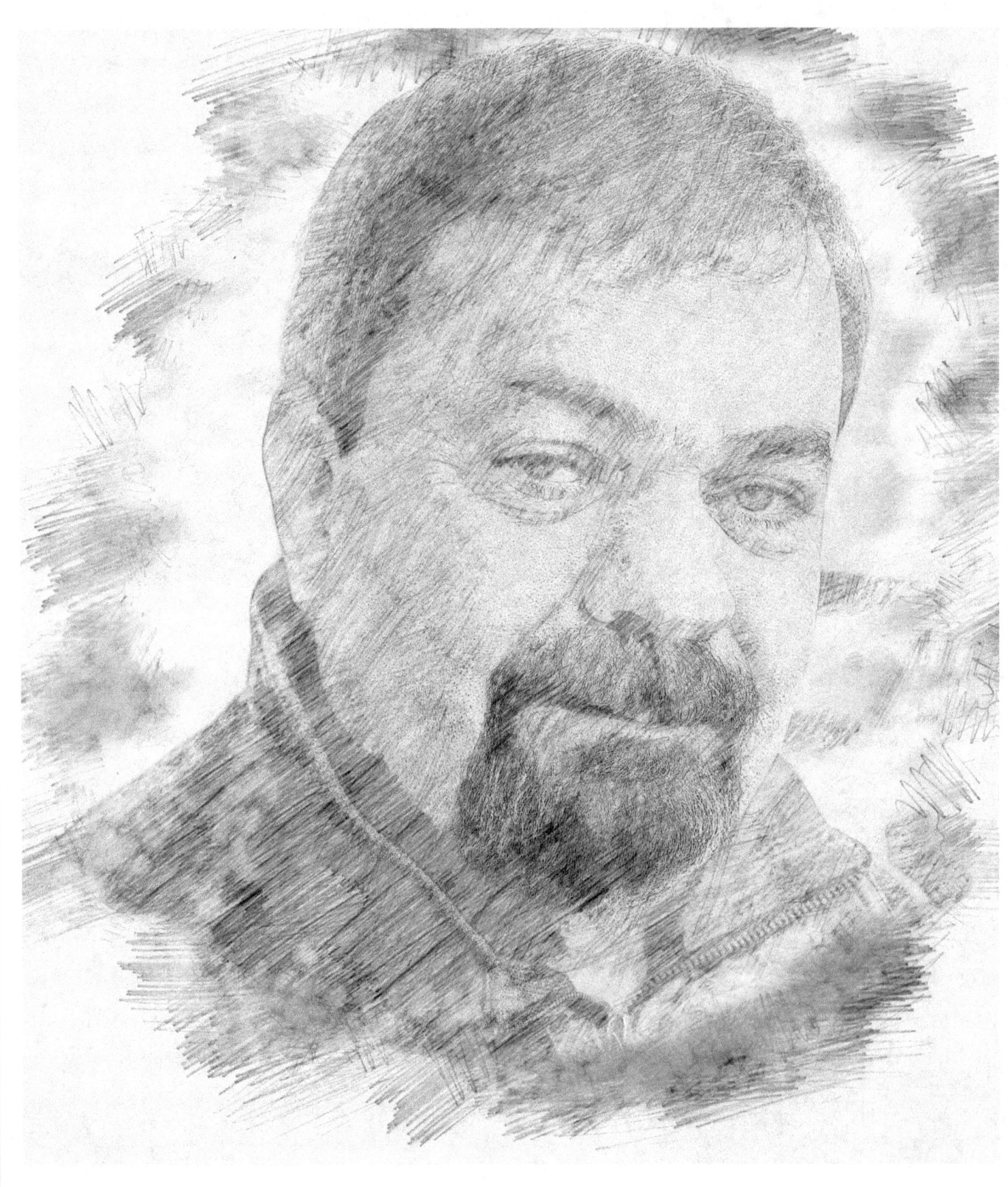

www.ingramcontent.com/pod-product-compliance
Lightning Source LLC
Chambersburg PA
CBHW082110220526
45472CB00009B/2126